THE SECOND COMING

BY

ZOLA LEVITT

ZOLA LEVITT

Zola Levitt is a Jewish believer thoroughly educated in the synagogues and brought to the Messiah in 1971. He holds degrees from Duquesne University, Indiana University and an honorary Th.D. from Faith Bible College. He has, in his Christian walk, addressed millions of people concerning the facts of the Bible through his national television program, **ZOLA LEVITT PRESENTS,** which is carried on the major Christian networks, CBN, PTL, TBN and LBN, and numerous large city broadcast stations.

Zola Levitt Ministries, Inc. is a teaching and evangelistic association guided by the standard of Rom. 1:16, "To the Jew first, and also to the Gentile." Like the apostle Paul, we work through the Gentiles to reach the Jews. We inform our Gentile viewers and listeners of those principles of the faith which will be most helpful to them in understanding and witnessing to their Jewish friends. Our ministry offers a wide variety of teaching materials including books, cassette tapes, music, video tapes, and some imported gift items from the Holy Land. A current list of these materials is available at no charge by writing to: ZOLA, Box 12268, Dallas, TX 75225.

ISBN 1-930749-33-3

THE SECOND COMING

FOREWORD

PROPHECY CAUSES TROUBLE

For some reason arguments, rivalries and downright losses of friendships always follow the controversial area of biblical prophecy. Differences sometimes still exist when a prophecy is actually fulfilled, as with the first coming of the Messiah or the 1948 restoration of Israel.

If there was controversy about the first coming of Jesus Christ, there is certainly more about the second. Though it is the return of the King that makes Christianity distinct from all other religions — though He clearly promised to come back for us (John 14:1-3) — the Second Coming remains one of the truly difficult issues in the Church today.

The surprising thing is that the Scriptures are extremely clear about prophecy in general and the Second Coming in particular. There are more books of the Bible dedicated purely to prophecy than any other single subject. There are exhaustive chapters dedicated to a prophetic theme and the return of the Messiah. The major chapters of the New Testament and the Gospels are very definitely prophetic and deal emphatically with this subject. As well, the final book of the Bible, Revelation, is clearly prophetic, and ends its message on a glorious note with the return of the "King of Kings" and "Lord of Lords."

The arguments seem to be over whether the Bible means what it literally says. And this book takes the position that it does. This book represents an attempt to clearly set down the details of the Second Coming of Jesus Christ precisely as described in the Scriptures.

WHAT SECOND COMING?

Just how one claims to be a Christian without believing in the return of Jesus Christ is, in the Apostle Paul's term, "a mystery." But the fact remains that a vast portion of what is known as the Christian Church today does not hold to a literal Second Coming.

The argument over Christ's return to troubled planet earth has roots going all the way back to St. Augustine of the 4th century. To this holy man of God and great church father, we owe much for many meaningful spiritual truths. However, Augustine utilized the system of interpretation of his day, Greek allegorism, in which a great deal of symbolism is read into the writing. He tended to depart from the obvious and literal meanings of key prophecies and to instead try to fit the conditions of his time into their meanings.

In his book, *The City of God*, Augustine saw the Church fulfilling all of the Old Testament prophecies made to the nation of Israel. When Augustine came to the word "Israel" he simply inserted the concept of the Church. When he read in the Old Testament that the Messiah would reign bodily in Jerusalem, he interpreted this as Christ now reigning in heaven over the Church on earth.

Augustine lived in the age of the coming glory of the Church. He magnified and exalted this institution even above what God had intended for it. He saw the nation of Israel and the kingdom promised to the Jewish people in the Old Testament as being fulfilled in the Church Age. He saw the nation of Israel banished from the presence of God forever!

This system of interpretation stripped the Bible, and especially prophecy, of its prime impact for hundreds of years. And even when the great reformers, such as Martin Luther and John Calvin, began to interpret the Bible literally again, they refused to touch upon or speak to the issue of prophecy.

Because of this historic aversion, most of our present-day denominations wallow in a sort of blindness and lack of understanding of prophetic truth. The theologians of most of the mainline denominational churches see nothing happening today that relates to biblical promises and prophecy.

Therefore, even the dramatic return of the nation of Israel to their land has no biblical or prophetic significance to them. And the thought of Christ returning bodily to establish a literal kingdom in Palestine becomes meaningless.

Since most of the mainline denominations are trained with this liberal view of the Bible, their concept of a Second Coming is virtually nonexistent. They say that Christ may someday return "in spirit," or that His righteousness may be apparent in every man when perfection is established on earth by social justice. But by no means do they have in view what the Scriptures really speak of — a literal, historic and bodily return of the resurrected Messiah to reign as King. Therefore, the majority of Christendom are totally blinded to this precious hope. The irony of it all is that Christ Himself, in His final and most important discourse, spoke volumes about His earthly return. But His voice and His words go unheeded in some circles.

Believers who take the Scriptures literally see the situation as a satanic plot to retard the central truth of Christianity from being proclaimed clearly to the lost and helpless generations.

WHEN WILL HE COME?

Even among those who believe in the literal return of the King, there are differing views about just when He will come. Those who accept the biblical concept of a thousand-year millennium, or earthly kingdom of God, still argue over whether the King will come before it or after it. Some Christians even hold that the Kingdom is already here.

POST-MILLENNIALISM. This view was very popular before World War I. Simply stated, it held that the Church by all its goodness and social graces would spread the good news of the Kingdom worldwide. With all these efforts the Church would pave the way for Christ's second coming. In other words, He would come only after the Church had "set up" the Kingdom.

But this viewpoint almost states that Christ needs human help to establish His own reign. In any case, when the millions began to die on the fields of Flanders during the great holocaust of 1914-18, this human virtue philosophy began to die off. Few today hold such an optimistic viewpoint on the goodness of the human race.

AMILLENNIALISM. Today, this is probably the most prevalent view in regard to the Second Coming of Christ. The word millennium, of course, is a Latin word that refers to one thousand, or, the one-thousand-year Kingdom reign of Christ. With the Greek "A", or negative, in front of this word, this view holds that there will be no millennium or earthly Kingdom. It adheres to what Augustine first began, and that is that the Church is the Kingdom. There will be no Kingdom in Israel to come with Israel's Messiah reigning. Most of the major denominations hold to this viewpoint. In a sense, there is a sort of pride and false view of the Church which prevails. "We are the Kingdom," says this self-righteous philosophy.

PRE-MILLENNIALISM. This viewpoint is growing by leaps and bounds. And in reality it is the most consistent and truthful view of the Scriptures. It sees all the Bible basically to be interpreted literally, including the area of biblical prophecy and future events. It therefore sees the subject of the Messiah's return to be taken at face value.

Many think this is a new viewpoint just arrived at over the last hundred years or so, but the fact that Israel's Messiah would come *before* the Kingdom to establish it was clearly the viewpoint of the early church fathers. We have unquestioned quotes from those who were closest to Jesus and the disciples that they expected a bodily, earthly return. Justin Martyr (100-168) was quite outspoken: "But I and whatsoever Christians are orthodox in all things do know there will be a resurrection of the flesh, in a thousand years in the city of Jerusalem,...according to what Ezekiel, Isaiah, and other prophets have promised."

He goes on to write, "A certain man among us, whose name is John, being one of the twelve apostles of Christ, in that revelation shown to him, prophesied, that those who believe in our Christ should fulfill a thousand years at Jerusalem; and after that the general, and in a word, the everlasting resurrection, and last judgment of all together."

Many other quotations could be cited, but this one is one of the most outstanding and authoritative statements made by the early church saints, and is plainly representative of their views.

THE FINAL WORD

One would expect the Jewish elders and rabbis — the great sages who spent their years studying Scripture as their life's work — to have a clear view of prophecy. And after all "they wrote the book". The Bible was entirely written and published in Israel by Jews. If we could demonstrate that the orthodox Jewish leaders looked for a literal and historical coming of the Messiah to reign and rule over the Kingdom in Israel, the issues would be more certain. Having no church to popularize, nor any other reason to "symbolize" the Scriptures, these ancient worthies would certainly have spoken truthfully to what they read in God's word.

What did the Jewish theologians of Jesus' time and the period of the second Temple think of this issue?

After years of study, the Jewish Historical Publications, Ltd. of Jerusalem published in 1977 an exhaustive treatment of the Jewish theological thought during and even before the period of Christ. To read this comprehensive work, *Society and Religion in the Second Temple Period, Volume I*, is to virtually settle the issue of how the Old Testament prophecies were understood. The Jews of before and during Christ's time clearly believed in a historical coming of the Messiah. They believed virtually everything we now see in the Old Testament. For example, the book states, "Of all people of antiquity, the people of Israel alone present the Messianic concept....For centuries, from the days of David to the end of the Second Temple period, the prophets developed and elaborated a broad complex of prophetic vision of the end of days and of the days of the Messiah."

The book goes on to speak of the popular biblical beliefs of Jesus' period. For example, they believed that Elijah would be the forerunner of the Messiah, proclaiming His coming and His turning the hearts of the fathers to their children and the hearts of the children to their fathers. The rabbis believed in a great trumpet sounding, called the Trumpet of the Messiah. They believed in a great war against Gog and Magog in which the King Messiah, offspring of the house of David, will be victorious and rule the world by His Holy Spirit. The rabbis went on and saw the knowledge of God, the God of Israel, spreading throughout the world.

They believed in a judgment seat from which the Messiah would judge the world and the righteous. And they clearly held that the expression, "The Son of Man" was referring to the Messiah. In fact, the book adds, "In this, the early rabbis were followed by the authors of the New Testament." They believed in the "birth pangs" of the Messiah which was another way of speaking of the great world tribulation. They saw the nation of Israel purged from its sin and restored to God. They believed the heavens would be shaken during this period of terror, and they saw the Davidic kingdom established by Him in His personal reign.

All of this points clearly to the subject and doctrine of the Second Coming. The ancient rabbis of Jesus' day understood the Old Testament prophecies as literal and historical. The early church fathers, as well, saw the chain of events of biblical prophecy the same way.

That's what this book is about...simply establishing what the Bible teaches in its most literal and explicit sense.

INTERPRETING PROPHECY

Scholars have developed methods of interpreting prophecy to avoid errors. With the advantage of hindsight, our being able to look back at prophecies already fulfilled, we can determine today the most accurate ways of considering those prophecies that concern our future. The interpretation of prophecy is an advanced theological science, not a matter of opinion or wishful thinking. When the principles are adhered to, the Scriptures give great reward to the serious student.

ISRAEL IS ISRAEL. In essence, understanding prophecy about the Second Coming is really simple. Without becoming too technical, we'd like to lay out some basic principles.

First of all, Israel is Israel! Now that sounds quite simple, but that is the heart of the whole matter in interpreting biblical prophecy. The words in the Bible mean what they say. Of course there are poetic utterances which must be taken as poetic, and most people have the understanding of that simple fact. But historical references dealing with nations, people and events can be seen quite clearly as literal, and taken as such.

For example, Jeremiah speaks of gathering Israel from all countries and bringing them again into the land and causing them to dwell safely there (Jeremiah 32:37). Anyone reading that passage would clearly see it as a prophetic reference to events to take place far beyond Jeremiah's time. And yet, some of the medieval church fathers took a reference like this to refer to the blessings of Christians in the Church Age. This is allergorizing the simple truth of Scripture.

Naturally, now that we see Israel actually regathered into their land, we have no need to read in some allegorical meaning about the Church. Obviously, Israel is Israel and the Church is the Church and those alive today can clearly see that they are separate things. The philosophy of the Church replacing Israel in the Scriptures still persists, however, purely by momentum it would seem.

THE FIRST VIEW IS THE MOST OBVIOUS. Another simple principle in interpreting prophecy is that the Scriptures should be most clear in the first reading. That is, the simple and most basic statements are the ones to begin with in interpreting a passage. This may not always be true, however; there can be exceptions. But the rule of thumb is to let the Scriptures speak for themselves. St. Augustine garbled the whole process by looking for hidden, mystical and allegorical meanings behind the obvious words of the Bible. This brought about confusion and a reluctance to simply take the Scriptures as written.

Obviously God did not issue to the human race a book which could not be understood as written.

A LITERAL BIBLE. Again, this simple principle simply reiterates the fact that our Bible is a historical book dealing with real and historical issues and people. When viewed as such, the book simply "flowers" and becomes meaningful.

Of course, there are certain books which need to be approached a little differently. There are five poetic books in the Scriptures: Job, Psalms, Proverbs, Ecclesiastes and Song of Solomon. Understanding this, we of course look for certain poetic images and utterances. But basically, most of the Bible is in a historical setting and should be taken literally.

When talking about the Second Coming of Jesus Christ, a simple illustration of the literal Bible principle can be seen in Acts 1:11. The angels make a very plain statement to the stunned apostles watching Christ ascend to the Father after His resurrection. "This same Jesus, who is taken up from you into Heaven, *shall so come in like manner* as you have seen Him go into Heaven (italic added)."

Clearly, the angels were referring to His historical and bodily appearance. They were not expecting merely the "spirit of Christ" to return and be labeled, "the Second Coming." The angels anticipated a *bodily* return.

Other examples in the New Testament fortify the literal meaning principle. Many times in the early chapters of Matthew, the author writes, "that it might be fulfilled which was spoken by the prophet." This is by way of stating, "Historically, certain events in the New Testament were fulfilled exactly as the prophets predicted." Matthew was adamant about this. Over and over again he uses this phrase.

Christ used the same principle in quoting the prophecies of the Old Testament. In Matthew 24:15, He says, "When you, therefore, shall see the abomination of desolation spoken of by Daniel the prophet..." His point is clear: When you see historically and literally that which was predicted...

In making another prophecy, Christ states, "Immediately after tribulation of those days shall the sun be darkened..." (24:29)

Other expressions are similar: "This generation shall not pass until all these things be fulfilled" (24:34).

"As the days of Noah were, so shall also the coming of the Son of Man be" (24:37).

"Watch, for you know not what hour your Lord does come" (24:42).

Concerning His Second Coming, in many ways Jesus spoke of a more literal, historic return than even all the prophets of the Old Testament. In Matthew we read: "For in such an hour as you think not, the Son of Man comes" (24:44).

"The Lord of that servant shall come in a day when he looks not for Him" (24:50).

"When the Son of Man shall come in His glory" (25:31).

Plainly it is a much more difficult task to allegorize or symbolize all of these direct statements by the Lord Himself than to simply take them at face value. He said He is coming, and by that we take it that He is coming. We have no good reason to suppose a deeper hidden meaning.

DOUBLE PROPHETIC REFERENCE. Many prophecies use what we call the Double Reference device. That is, in one context two very different and distinct predictions may be seen. But there can be a gap of hundreds or thousands of years between the two events.

One of the more striking examples is in Zechariah 9:9-10. In verse 9, there is a prediction of Christ entering Jerusalem and heralded as a king riding upon an ass during His first coming, or first advent. But verse 10 really speaks of His second coming, to "speak peace among the nations; and His dominion shall be from sea even to sea and from the River even unto the end of the earth."

The principle is simple. Verse 9 speaks of His first coming in which He came to die as our sacrifice. Verse 10 speaks of

His Second Coming in which He will bring righteousness and peace to the entire world.

Another example of double reference is Isaiah 11:1-3. In verse 1, the origins and birth of the Messiah are spoken of. He is called the Branch who shall grow up out of the stem of Jesse, who was David's father. But verses 2-5 refer to His righteous and peaceful reign. In other words, verse 1 was fulfilled at His first coming; He was of that lineage. The remaining verses will be fulfilled at His second coming, as He rules. The purpose of the first verse was to unquestionably identify the Messiah, and the rest of the passage speaks of His greater mission. We note that the entire Church Age falls between the two comings, but this is of no consequence. From where we stand in time we have seen the first coming but obviously have not as yet seen the second. We are aware from these double reference prophecies there is more to come from the King. And after all, isn't that what our faith is all about?

The double reference principle is seen again in Isaiah 61:1-2. In fact, Christ Himself authorized this double reference device when He spoke at the synagogue at Nazareth quoting this very passage from Isaiah (Luke 4:16-21). Isaiah 61:1 refers to the Messiah being anointed by the Lord and the Spirit to bring good tidings to the meek. In the synagogue, Christ ended the reading of this passage with the phrase, "to proclaim the acceptable year of the Lord," verse 2. He did not complete the rest of verse 2 which spoke of the "day of vengeance", which would be the coming tribulation. In other words, Christ saw these two events as broken by His death and our present age. At some future time the "day of vengeance" will take place.

To understand that the Second Coming of Jesus Christ is a literal and historic event is foundational to this study. The basic issue is whether we believe the plain words of the Scriptures. If we do, we can believe without question in His Second Coming.

THE SETTING FOR
THE SECOND COMING

PRESENT-DAY EVENTS

Without question it would take a hermit to deny that our world is moving to the brink of a terrible event or events which will bring on a great world tribulation. Our newspapers and magazines are filled with ominous signs.

Something drastic will have to take place soon. The world is faced with a shortage of fuel, a still-exploding over-population and nuclear proliferation. As well, the Arab-Israeli tension could be the spark which throws the world into the predicted chaos. The Jewish rabbis before the time of Christ understood that such a world tribulation would herald the ultimate coming of the Messiah. All indicators are that we are now in this era.

None of us wishes to be a prophet or to try to predict something we are not clear on. But without question, within the next 5 to 50 years, something dramatic will take place on the world scene.

Our global situation heralds such a collision course.

NEWSWEEK MAGAZINE: "Why We Must Act Now"

"Perhaps most important, America's political will and spirit will erode, pitting citizens against citizens in an age of energy scarcity."

TIME MAGAZINE: "The World Over a Barrel"

"In all this rising tension, Russia is acting as a catalyst in the Middle East sore spot."

NEWSWEEK MAGAZINE: "So long as Muammer Kaddafi can hold on to his position as Libya's Teacher-Leader, the Russian's major link to the Arab world will remain secure."

ALEXANDER SOLZHENITSYN: "Over the last two years, terrible things have happened. The West has given up all its world positions.

"I wouldn't be surprised at the sudden and imminent fall of the West.

"There was a time at the beginning of the '50's, when this nuclear threat hung over the world. But the attitude of the West was like granite, and the West did not yield. Today this nuclear threat still hangs over both sides, but the West has chosen the wrong path of making concessions."

HAROLD BROWN, SECRETARY OF DEFENSE: "If the Soviets continue to build up military capability relative to us — then I think the situation five years down the road could be a serious one."

GENERAL ALEXANDER HAIG: "The enemy is moving. The big Russian build-up is part of a strategy of worldwide imperialism. We are getting to the fine edge of disaster."

GEORGE F. WILL, NEWSWEEK MAGAZINE: "Most Americans, including their leaders, cannot bring themselves to think that Soviet leaders are planning for the 'unthinkable' but all Americans should at least wonder."

Without question, we live in very troubled and tense days. All these signs point to the end times. The end times point to the Second Coming of Israel's Messiah. There are ominous indicators that should tell us things are moving to some grand conclusion.

INDICATORS OF THE FINAL HOUR

There are many indicators that we are at the end of world history as we know it. Below are some listed factors which point to that fact:

1. Israel's return to the land. The prophets made it clear that when Israel's king comes there will be regathered Jews in the land who will have established the nation of Israel.

2. Man's ability to destroy the world (Rev. 8:7-11, 6:8). The Book of Revelation and other Scriptures speak of a worldwide holocaust. The passages in that final book speak of a third of the world's forests being consumed and all the green grass being burned. It's only been recently, within our times, that such events have become feasible.

3. A near-world economic collapse with accompanying world inflation (Rev. 6:5-8). In this passage in Revelation, there is a terrible and massive world inflation whereby a person will work all day long simply to buy a loaf of bread.

4. To have world starvation and economic ruin *implies* a massive world population which cannot feed itself. The whole tone of the Book of Revelation and the terrors that are coming on the earth point to an interlocked and massive population which is virtually helpless during the coming reign of terror.

5. The rise of the revised Roman Empire from ten parts or ten nations. The European Common Market now has nine nations with Greece applying to be the tenth* (Dan. 7:7-8).

6. The Arab Confederation allied with Russia against Israel (Ezek. 38:5-6).

7. The upsurge of the occult and demon activity (I Tim. 4:1; Rev. 9:20-21).

THE WORLD HOLOCAUST. There are two phenomena which *specifically* herald the Second Coming of Christ — Israel's return to the land and this coming world tribulation.

*Greece was approved in January, 1981. The ten nation confederacy is now complete.

The "tribulation" we spoke of in Matthew 24-26 will be the rushing together of all the above international forces. This period of terror will last seven years, with the last three and one-half years being the most horrible. The Book of Revelation gives us a program of events:

1. Peace taken from the earth, 6:4
2. Massive starvation, 6:1-6
3. Plague and famine, 6:8
4. Great shaking of the earth, 6:12-17
5. Jewish witnesses slain, 7:1-17
6. World nearly totally destroyed, 8:7-11
7. A world dictator deceiving the nations, 13
8. The seas polluted, 16:3-4

Rapidly, the appearance of these factors is more and more evident. What could, or will, trigger the presence of these events?

THE EVENTS OF
THE SECOND COMING

THE PROPHETIC SCENARIO

THE RAPTURE OF THE CHURCH. If we were to paint a portrait of the events leading to the Second Coming of Christ, we would have to begin with the Rapture of the Church. The key passage is I Thessalonians 4:13-5:9. The Rapture, or the catching up to heaven of the believers, precedes the earthly tribulation and holocaust.

It is not the purpose of this book to treat exhaustively the subject of the Rapture. (We would recommend Zola Levitt's Glory: The Future of the Believers, or Raptured for further study.) Toward the end of this book, we will make a comparison of the Rapture and the Second Coming.

Believers are guaranteed a liberation from the tribulation to come. We have listed some of the predicted indicators which point us to the end times. There are still other events given as prior to Jesus' return. And with our situation of world turmoil today, we can reasonably construct a scenario of the end.

As already mentioned, the world will have been seven years into what is called the Tribulation when the Lord returns to reign. Christ speaks in no uncertain terms about this period of terror in Matthew 24:21-28. He describes this seven years as the worst period in world history: "There shall be great tribulation such as was not since the beginning of the world to this time, no nor ever shall be. Except those days should be shortened, there should no flesh be spared."

The Book of Revelation sees a fourth of the world's population destroyed at one time during this terrible period!

If we were going to try to analyze what causes this nightmare on earth, we could draw a pretty complete picture from what we know of present-day world events. Things could go something like this:

In the next few years the world could truly run out of its oil supplies. In fact, in the 1980 s, Russia will have depleted her known reserves. As each year passes and the world supplies diminish, we can easily picture a soaring demand for the black gold. In time, smaller, less secure nations will begin to crumble economically. Worldwide recession would set in, and in time begin to affect larger areas such as America, Europe and Russia.

Meanwhile, Russia will have courted the Middle East Arab countries in order to secure oil and cut off supplies to the West. Red China, a growing industrial nation, also needs further oil supplies. She will begin to make moves toward the Middle East.

Tension mounts. The worldwide weapons system becomes more sophisticated and deadly. Because of inner turmoil in some Arab countries, Russia makes blatant moves with troops and reinforcements. America calls her hand and moves troops and ships into the Middle East. The European powers must now arm, because they will stand or fall with the United States.

Recession turns into worldwide depression. There are bread lines and food riots. To secure oil, Russia makes a military move. The U.S. counters by limited land and sea forces. There's an exchange of short-range nuclear attacks. The world goes on alert as the Arabs use this time of turmoil to attack Israel.

We can picture step by step, though not really knowing details, of the world falling into the tribulation trap. Since the Church will have been raptured as these events begin, there will be little spiritual life to hold back the forces of evil now in control.

NATURE IN UPHEAVAL. As nuclear attacks are exchanged, thousands are dying in the cities. Though the major powers can destroy each other a dozen times over, they are releasing rockets on a limited and strategic basis. The seas and rivers are polluted, the forests are destroyed. And in the process the balance of nature is completely toppled. Christ refers to this awful time in Luke 21:25-26.

"And there shall be signs in the sun, and in the moon, and in the stars; and upon the earth distress of the nations, mixed with perplexity; the sea and the waves roaring; men's hearts failing them for fear and for looking after the things coming on the earth; for the powers of heaven shall be shaken."

Massive pollution will probably cover the earth's atmosphere. Strong gale-like winds, possibly earthquakes and volcanos, will add to the terror. The climate will be affected, and the seas will spill over their shores.

The world will be terrified because of the things coming on the earth.

ISRAEL IN AGONY. With all the events of the tribulation swirling about the globe, the nation of Israel lies at the vortex of the wrath of mankind. Little Israel will again be the scapegoat for all the earth's ills. The prophet Zechariah makes it clear that as the tribulation moves to a climax, the powers that be will sweep over that small, defenseless country. The Jews will probably fight a gallant fight, but alone they by no means are capable of handling the combined forces of the nations.Zechariah warns what God will do when the nations move against tiny Israel (2:8-9): "For he that touches you (Israel) touches the pupil of His (God's) eye. For, behold, I will shake my hand upon them (the nations)." God considers the Jewish people and the city of Jerusalem like the pupil of His eye. When the nations move against Israel, God will move against the nations!

But in this swirl of the tribulation events, humanly speaking, the little nation of Israel will seem to be facing extinction. Zechariah talks about this: "For I will gather all nations against Jerusalem to battle; and the city shall be taken, and the houses spoiled, and the women ravaged; and half of the city shall go forth in captivity," (14:2).

"Then shall the Lord go forth and fight against these nations, as when He fought in the day of battle" (14:3). Many in the city of Jerusalem and the nation of Israel will have died. But at the very end, the Lord will return to spare the remnant of His people. Those that will be spared, we believe, are those who have trusted God during this terrible period.

1. *Christ, Israel's Messiah, Returns Instantly.* As the prophet Zechariah is describing the destruction of Israel, he turns immediately to describe the lightning-like return of Israel's Messiah to spare His people (Zech. 14:4, 12:10-11). The prophet utters some of the most remarkable verses in the Old Testament. He pictures the feet of the Messiah, on that day of His return, on the Mount of Olives.

When the Messiah's feet touch this small hill, an earthquake will take place and a great valley will be formed as the mountain is torn in half.

The nation of Israel and the world will know that He has returned!

Without a world of doubt, the world will know who *He* is. The prophet wrote that God would "pour upon the house of David, and upon the inhabitants of Jerusalem, the spirit of grace and of supplications; and they shall look upon me whom they have pierced, and they shall mourn for him, as one mourns for his only son, and there shall be bitterness for him as one who is in bitterness for his firstborn. And in that day there shall be a great mourning in Jerusalem" (12:10-11).

To all Jewish commentators, this is a terribly embarrassing passage. The medieval Jewish rabbis, in their honesty, admit that the one with the pierced hands is the Messiah. His hands, of course, were pierced at His first coming when He was crucified and died for the sins not only of Israel but of the world. The nation of Israel and the Jewish people will recognize that the one they slew was truly their King and Messiah. They will cry and weep in great bitterness in recognizing Him.

Christ, in Matthew 24, alludes to this truth of His return and sudden appearance. He says, "For as the lightning comes out of the east and shines even into the west, so also shall the coming of the Son of Man be." As lightning flashes across the entire sky, it appears to be an instant discharge; so the coming of Christ shall be. His return will be dramatic, instant and seen by the world. In fact, in verse 30, He makes it clear that when He comes, "all the tribes of the earth shall mourn, and they shall see the Son of Man coming in clouds. . .with power and great glory."

Can you imagine the shock and disbelief of the world that has virtually denied His very existence? Now they must face the fact of His reality and His literal return to deliver His people, Israel.

2. *The Tribulation Is Stopped.* With His instant return, peace which has so long eluded mankind is quickly brought to planet earth. The Bible does not give us exact details as to how the Messiah executes this peace. Maybe it's through His accompanying angels or the returned saints who execute His authority. However, this peace is accomplished

instantly, and on a worldwide basis.

Again, the prophet Zechariah speaks of this coming peace as universal. As in Zechariah 9:9, he spoke of the first coming of the King when He presented Himself upon the donkey before Jerusalem; in verse 10 the prophet tells of the battle bow being cut off and the Messiah speaking peace to all the nations. He adds, "His dominion shall be from sea even to sea and from the River even to the ends of the earth."

Because the holocaust or tribulation has been worldwide, only the King of Kings can bring about a world peace. The Bible pictures the tribulation as true terror never before known. Can you imagine the blessing of this peace that stops the horrible carnage among nations?

Yearly, the U.S. and the United Nations spend billions trying to stop wars and create treaties to guarantee worldwide peace. In the end, the world fails again. Only the Second Coming of God's Son to earth can bring about the peace man has so longed for.

3. *National and Personal Judgment.* One of the first things that the Messiah must do upon His dramatic return to the earth is separate the remaining powerful forces which were clashing against each other on the earth. He must separate the nations, and the individuals, on the basis of their trust and their commitment. For the Bible declares that there will be those who have turned to God even during this terrible period. But the majority of mankind will have died in gnashing anger against God. The military forces that are left alive will have aligned themselves against the nation of Israel, and the King must pass sentence. In Matthew 25:32-46, the judgment of the nations is described. At first glance, this judgment is made on a peculiar basis. Verse 32 tells us that He gathers all nations together and divides them as a shepherd divides the sheep from the goats. The sheep are placed on His right hand, the goats on His left.

The basis of the judgment is the treatment of "my brothers," (vs. 40). The criteria is whether those judged shared their provisions and food and water with His brethren. If one studies the context carefully, the "brothers" are the Jewish people who are being slaughtered and persecuted during this period. And to align oneself with the Jewish people is a true and open expression of faith and trust in God. This faith will be rewarded by the King and Judge (Gen. 12:3). Israel, even in the tribulation, will stand as a monument and a test to the peoples of the earth.

For those who in vile hatred mistreated Israel, there is capital punishment, the death sentence, verse 46: "And these shall go away into eternal punishment but the righteous into life eternal."

Somehow, God will divide His judgment between the nations, their national and international policies, and the individuals. The King will do this with perfect righteousness. Revelation 19:15 further describes this judgment of the nations. It says that out of the Messiah's mouth will go a sharp sword, and with it He will smite the nations and rule with a rod of iron.

Christ will not only judge the nations, but He will create legal and authoritative boundaries to control those remaining even in the coming Kingdom. Righteousness and judgment will be absolute during His reign. Only the Son of God could bring this perfect justice. A human ruler is susceptible to bribery and fallible judgment, but Christ will judge with perfect equality both the nations and individuals.

4. *Judgment of the Satanic Forces.* The Bible is book-ended by a promise and fulfillment of a promise, both of which deal directly with the forces and power of evil, Satan himself. In Genesis 3:15 we have the promise of judgment upon this personality, Lucifer, who embodies himself in the temptation serpent: "And I will put emotional enmity between you (Satan) and the woman, and between your

seed and her seed; he (the seed of the woman) shall crush your head (Satan), and you shall crush his heel." Embodied in this cryptic passage is the promise of future judgment against this powerful being. The promise is stored away in a very literal and historic event, the encounter between mankind and Satan. The Bible is the story of God's redemption and His preparation for the judgment of this personality. The prophecy is fulfilled in the last few chapters of the Bible. In Revelation 20:2, the Messiah lays hold of the dragon: "that old serpent, who is the devil and Satan, and bound him a thousand years." He is then cast into the bottomless pit, and it is sealed in order that he would not be able to deceive the nations again.

He is released after the thousand-year reign of the Messiah. The description of the final hours of Satan is given in abbreviated form in Revelation 20. The outline is simple and concise:

1. He's arrested and bound by the Messiah for a thousand years, vs. 2.

2. He is cast into a place of confinement, vs. 3.

3. He will be released following the thousand-year millennium reign of the Messiah in which he will deceive the nations again, vs. 3; vs. 7.

4. He will again promote an international spiritual deception of the nations. He will rally some of the ancient ancestors of Israel's earlier enemies, Gog and Magog, vs. 8.

5. Satan will march on Jerusalem, capital of the Messiah, but his insurrection will be stopped immediately, vs. 9.

6. Satan will be cast into a place of confinement and torment for eternity, vs. 10.

Along with this judgment, a sentence is passed as well on the Antichrist of the tribulation and the false religious leader (Rev. 19:20). Together with Satan, these two, the most powerful and evil men of world history, are cast into eternal judgment (20:10).

The only logical answer we have for the confining and then the release of Satan is that the Kindgom period of Revelation 20 is, in a sense, a final test of the heart and will of mankind. For though the thousand-year reign of Christ is a near-perfect state, the heart of man will still be at work. Though men will see and enjoy Christ reigning in Jerusalem, the sense of rebellion and independence will still come to the fore. When Satan is released, he will find ripe ground for an insurrection. This Kindgom test will demonstrate that the heart of man, too, is wicked.

5. *Nature and Disease are Controlled.* When Jesus comes, He creates a near-perfect environment. We know from the book of Ezekiel that there will still be death and human judgment. Man's sin nature will still be around, though Satan is confined. But, too, the Messiah will have control over the natural world. Disease will be thwarted. Medical science will be unlocked and will never be more perfect than under His reign. Many passages of the Old Testament prophetically suggest idyllic scenes and we've selected a few for illustration. Isaiah 11:6-8 claims the wolf will lie down with the lamb, and the leopard will lie down with the small goat. Children will lead about the lion as well as the calf. The bear and the cow will feed together. And small nursing children will play by the snake's den and not be harmed.

Few commentators take this as poetic. Most see these statements as genuinely reflecting a change in the nature of the animal kingdom.

Most know of the passages speaking of the desert blossoming as a rose. This is set forth in Isaiah 35, but the passage also adds that the weak hands will be strengthened, the eyes of the blind will be opened, and the ears of the deaf will be unstopped.

There will be miraculous cures under the administration of the Messiah. Since the New Testament claims that He

Himself made us and controls the very course of the natural world, such cures and healings would certainly be effective.

As well, agriculture will be increased, especially in the land of Israel: "The desolate land shall be tilled. . . this land that was destined to become like the Garden of Eden," Ezekiel 36:34-35. God adds, "And I will multiply the fruit of the tree, and the increase of the field, that you shall receive no more reproach of famine among the nations" (Ezekiel 36:30).

These things don't just happen to be empty, miraculous signs. They are testimonies to the person of the Messiah and His power. Though the Arab world at the present is virtually at war with Israel, the remaining people surrounding Israel will be especially blessed: "the nations left round about you shall know that I, the Lord, build the ruined places and plant that which was desolate" (Ezekiel 36:36).

Can you imagine such a world in which there is near absolute harmony between nature and the realm of mankind? But this is exactly what the Old Testament proclaims will happen. The peace that He will bring, though not absolute, will be the nearest thing to natural perfection in the physical world as we know it. But in spite of all the beauty and productivity that God will bring about, the hearts of some men will still be restless and unappreciative of what God's Son will be doing.

6. *The Davidic Kingdom Will Be Restored.* Jeremiah 30:3 in plain and understandable language speaks of the historical restoration of the Jews back to the land: "I will save you Israel from afar. . . then Jacob shall return and be at rest and be quiet" (30:10).

In loving-kindness, God will draw Israel back to the land (31:3). The Lord will save His people, the remnant of Israel, and "bring them from the north country and gather them from the furthest part of the earth" (31:7-8).

Even though Israel has been unfaithful, God will be faithful concerning its restoration. The prophecies uttered by Jeremiah were first spoken by Moses in Deuteronomy 30. Moses made it very clear that "the Lord your God will turn back your captivity, and have compassion upon you, and will return and gather you from all nations, where the Lord your God has scattered you." The Jewish people will again possess the land of their fathers.

Jeremiah makes it clear that God will cause the Jews to dwell safely in the land. The Jews will not go back with a cold heart, but their eyes will be opened when they see the Messiah and God will, "give them one heart, and one way that they may fear me forever" (Jer. 32:39). God will "plant them in this land assuredly with my whole heart and my whole soul" (32:41).

In ancient times few but the nomads inhabited the desert of Israel, but there is a strange prophecy in Jeremiah which predicts that cities will be planted in the Negev, or the desert (32:44).

All these promises about restoration, fruitfulness and blessing have slowly begun. We call this the "beginning of the beginnings," not the actual fulfillment, but, in a sense, the anticipation of that fulfillment. Cities are now being planted in the Negev and the Jews have turned the rocky, dried up land into a place flowing with milk and honey.

We are near the predicted fulfillment and the Second Coming of Israel's Messiah!

Daniel 7:13-14 makes it clear that all this will be taking place because the Son of Man, the Messiah, will receive the promised Kingdom; and that Kingdom will not be destroyed nor pass away. All rabbinical commentaries point to the fact that Daniel 7:13-14 is distinctly messianic, and that the expression 'Son of Man' refers to the Messiah. In Christ's day, we know that the scholarly rabbis understood the expression 'Son of Man' as referring to deity. They knew that His Kingdom was the Kingdom promised to David.

Revelation 20:2 speaks of this Davidic Kingdom as lasting a thousand years. The amillenial scholars see this expression, 'thousand years', as figurative language—that the Kingdom is something mystical and cryptic, not literal and historical. However, examining the passages in Revelation 20, it's clear that a distinct time period is to be understood. Satan is "bound a thousand years." He is not released "until a thousand years are completed." The saints "live and reign with Christ a thousand years." And, "the rest of the dead live not again until the thousand years are finished." And finally, "when the thousand years are ended, Satan shall be loosed out of his prison."

This thousand-year reign of Christ is clearly a distinct time on the calendar. It has a beginning and end, and specified events within this time period.

Besides all the things we have so far listed about the Kingdom reign of the Messiah, there is one promise concerning the land of Egypt that is startling. Isaiah 19:16-25 predicts that Egypt, as well as the people of Assyria, will be blessed during the Kingdom reign of Christ. We have always thought of Egypt as the prime enemy of Israel, and historically this has been so. But this prophecy makes it clear that Egypt will someday be forgiven and blessed.

Before our very eyes, in our own time, we have seen peace come between Israel and Egypt. We believe this is a foreshowing of the Kingdom blessing. It could well be that millions of Egyptians will someday know the Lord and trust Israel's Messiah. The prophecy in Isaiah 19 speaks of the Egyptians knowing the language of Canaan and swearing an oath to the Lord of Hosts. In fact, on the borders between Egypt and Israel, a pillar (a monument or altar) will be set up for the Lord. "And it shall be for a sign and for a witness, unto the Lord of Hosts in the land of Egypt" (vs. 20).

Even more startling is the statement, "He (the Lord) shall send them a Savior, and a great one, and He shall deliver them. And the Lord shall be known in Egypt and the Egyptians shall know the Lord in that day" (vs. 20b, 21).

The passage goes on to describe how the Lord will heal the Egyptian people. A highway will pass from Egypt through Israel to Assyria, and the three countries will virtually form one nation (vs. 24).

The borders of the Davidic Jewish Kingdom will be from the River of Egypt to the Euphrates, according to God's promise to Abraham in Genesis 15:18. This would tie in with the prophecy in Isaiah 19 in which the Kingdom borders will include Syria and Egypt.

7. *The Temple is Restored in Jerusalem.* Ezekiel 40-47 has been regarded by many scholars as a strange prophecy. It is actually the description of the millennial Temple in Jerusalem. The passage is rather detailed, depicting an entirely new building and function as never before seen in the rest of the Bible.

Critics have faulted those who believe the passage is speaking of the millennial Temple. But clearly, its purposes are different than the old Temple built during Solomon's day. Though sacrifices are offered, it seems as if these are but memorial offerings looking back on the sacrifice of the Messiah. Because of this, some of the rituals are different, and prescribed in different language than in the prescription for the past Temples.

The priesthood of the millennial Temple is also somewhat different. The priests who are to function in the new Temple are to be of the house of Zodok, and not all the Levites in general (44:15).

In this section there is continual reference to the Prince, the 'nasi' in Hebrew. He is mentioned extensively in chapters 45-46. The whole land is His personal possession (45:8). All Jewish commentators believe this clearly describes the Messiah. And though He is of the house of David and not of the earthly priesthood, He will present offerings to the Lord. Only the Messiah could have this right and power. In chapter 45:21-22, this Prince prepares for Himself and His people an offering. He also will make offerings during the period of Passover. This seems to clearly answer what Christ had in mind in Matthew 26:29 when He told His disciples, "I will not drink henceforth of this fruit of the vine, until the day I drink it new with you in my father's kingdom." The drink He was referring to was of course, the Passover cup. Jesus must be that Prince of the new kingdom Temple.

8. *The Finale of World Resistance.* At the close of the formal Kingdom Age, the one-thousand-year reign, Satan will be loosed from his prison and there will follow a formal insurrection against the Messiah reigning in Jerusalem (Revelation 20:7-10). This passage is rather abbreviated and contains little detail, as we've seen above. Because the hearts of some men are still evil even in this near-perfect state, there is a rebellion against the Messiah's authority and rule. But it is short-lived, and when the followers of Satan come against Israel and encircle the beloved city of Jerusalem, God sends fire from heaven which devours them instantly.

This is the last stroke of earthly judgment performed by God upon earthly humanity. Though the verses which follow in this chapter of Revelation speak of a Great White Throne Judgment, mankind in its present state will never again be judged by God.

Many have asked the identity of those in Revelation 20:8-9 that rebel against Christ. Most have always thought the Kingdom will be inhabited by perfect and regenerated people. But actually, there are two classes of human beings who live and exist in the Kingdom. There are the saints of all ages who enter the Kingdom in their new, glorified and resurrected bodies. They will be sinless and unaffected by temptation and rebellion. But there will be those who are saved during the tribulation who enter the Kingdom in their natural human bodies. They will have children, who have children, who have children, etc. The third, fourth and fifth generation of children, though living in a perfect setting and knowing of the Messiah in Israel, will still have rebellious hearts. They will decide of their own volition that they do not want Christ, and they will be ready victims for this insurrection staged by Satan against the Messiah. It is they who will be destroyed when they confront Him in Jerusalem.

9. *The Judgment Seat of the Messiah.* Revelation 20:11-15 describes the Great White Throne of Judgment. This follows the formal Kingdom period and is the judgment of all unregenerated dead from all ages. The passage describes the sea and the earth giving up the dead for judgment.

We know that men are saved by their faith and trust in Jesus Christ personally (John 3:16). But at this Great White Throne Judgment, men will be judged by their works. In a sense there are two ways of coming to God, by faith and by works. Those who come to God by works will not make it, because their works will condemn them, not save them.

In this passage two sets of books are described. The "book of life" and "the books". If those standing before God are not recorded in the Book of Life, God will open the books and judge them by their works. The passage makes it clear there is no second chance. Those not found written in the Book of Life will be judged and condemned.

This is a terrifying passage of Scripture. Final judgment is a very negative thought to ponder, but it only amplifies the love and grace of God in His Son. God has ingeniously devised a way whereby our sins were passed to His Son, and thereby condemned and judged. By placing our faith in Him, we do not have to face this condemnation. He represented us at the cross, and we are identified by faith in

His death, burial and resurrection. Thereby, our sins were punished, but our souls and spirits are left free to know God eternal. God asks but one thing of us, trust. This is what we call 'amazing grace'. God completely worked out the mechanics of our salvation, and we do not have to face eternal damnation.

We have looked at most but not all the events of the Second Coming and resulting Kingdom. Again, as we stated in the beginning, we believe the time is very near. Soon God will do something very distinct and dramatic. The world will soon fall into a great period of darkness which will usher in the tribulation. And as the Jewish rabbis put it, this tribulation heralds the coming of the Messiah.

We pray, Lord, soon for Your coming!

DISTINGUISHING THE RAPTURE
AND
THE SECOND COMING

THE PROBLEM. There is a problem which has been causing continual confusion in the minds of students of the Bible. It is distinguishing the doctrines of the Rapture and the Second Coming. Many do not understand the Scriptures thoroughly enough to see that two wholly distinct issues are described. This chapter will attempt to show the distinction between these two great truths.

The best way to examine how these doctrines work together and yet are distinct is to find out what they really and truly are. What is the Rapture? And specifically, what is the Second Coming of Christ?

THE RAPTURE QUESTION

Let's first examine the Rapture question. The main passage of Scripture for the Rapture is found in I Thessalonians 4:13-5:9. Below are some of the distinguishing points of what the Rapture is about:

1. It deals with those who are "asleep", or have died trusting Jesus, vs. 13.

2. And it has to do with those who are alive, vs. 17.

3. Paul begins spelling out this truth by telling his readers at the church of Thessalonica that he did not want them to be ignorant about the subject, vs. 14. By this he is implying

that they knew nothing of this subject previously.

4. Paul speaks of Jesus bringing those who are asleep when He comes back, vs. 14. These are saints who have previously died. When Jesus comes, He will bring their souls with Him.

5. The Lord will return with shouts from heaven, vs. 16.

6. The dead in Christ (the Messiah) will rise first, vs. 16.

7. Then, *we* who are alive and remain will be caught up with Him in the clouds to meet the Lord in the air, vs. 17.

8. This "catching up" is referred to in Latin as *raptura,* thus we get the term "rapture", vs. 17.

9. Notice that the living believers and those who are asleep will be caught up to meet Christ in the air, vs. 17. This is clearly not the Lord coming to reign on earth.

10. Paul goes on and says that the believers reading this letter know perfectly well about the "day of the Lord", 5:1-2. Now the apostle Paul has shifted his subject. The day of the Lord is *not* the Rapture, for he states clearly that they know of the day of the Lord and they knew nothing about the Rapture. The day of the Lord is an Old Testament phrase referring to two things. . . the terror of the coming tribulation and the return of the Lord as the judge. There are some 25 references in the Old Testament to this phrase. None of the references describes anything like the Rapture in chapter 4.

11. Paul says that they, the world, will find sudden destruction coming upon them and they will not escape, vs. 3.

12. "But you, brothers, (the Christians) are not in darkness that that day will overcome you as a thief," vs. 4.

13. "For God has not appointed us to wrath, but to obtain deliverance by our Lord Jesus Christ," vs. 9.

14. In I Corinthians 15, Paul speaks of all believers not

facing death but all believers will be "changed", vs. 51.

15. This change will happen instantly, vs. 52.

16. Paul calls this change a mystery. In other words, a truth not revealed before in the Old Testament.

SUMMARY: We've described the key points about what the Rapture actually is. It has nothing to do with the Lord coming down to earth to reign. Now let's look at what the Second Coming actually is.

WHAT IS THE SECOND COMING?

1. It is a literal and historical, earthly reign in Israel and Jerusalem.

2. It is the bodily return of Jesus Christ to the earth.

3. It is not described as a mystery or something that believers knew nothing of. It is a reign of peace that will extend worldwide.

4. It occurs at the end of the seven-year tribulation.

Confusion Concerning the Rapture and the Second Coming. The expression "the day of the Lord so comes as a thief in the night," (I Thess. 5:2), has caused many problems in theological circles. The day of the Lord is in reference to the Second Coming, not the Rapture. And the expression, "thief in the night" has so often been applied to the Rapture, but it really has to do with the Second Coming and the reign of terror and judgment on the unbelievers. Note also in I Thess. 5:3 that the unbelievers shall not escape this terror and wrath to come. That certainly is not speaking of the believer, who is to be taken out and rescued.

There has been much confusion over Matthew 24, vs. 36-51, as well. So many apply this passage to the Rapture. But there are many reasons why this could not be so.

First of all, the context of the message is a warning by the

King of the Jews to His subjects. We should study the Bible by what's going on at the moment, chapter by chapter. In the Olivet Discourse, which runs from Matthew 24 through 26, Jesus is talking about the terrible times to come upon the nation of Israel. He in no way alludes to the Church. The point of the whole passage is coming judgment, not the res cue of believers.

One of the key verses in this section is verse 37, "but as the days of Noah were, so shall also the coming of the son of man be." The days of Noah were days of impending judgment. People went on about their daily lives as if nothing was going to happen (vs. 38-39). There is a warning in this passage to "Watch. . . for you know not what hour your Lord does come" (vs. 42). But in the context Jesus is talking to the nation of Israel, and the ones being snatched away are taken to judgment, not to heaven to be with Him, (vs. 40-41). The unfaithful servant in the passage is the Jew who is not looking for his Messiah. Because the times and the issues are so severe, the unfaithful servant is executed (vs. 51).

This description of judgment is certainly not for believers today. The Rapture is a glorious liberation from planet earth, prior to great destruction and wrath (I Thess. 5:9). Judgment is certainly not the "blessed hope" of the believer.

Another great demonstration of the deliverance provided by the Rapture is found in the total organization of the Book of Revelation. The Church is not mentioned from chapter 4 on, as the apostle John describes "the things to come," in all their horror. Instead, we see a group of believers in heaven enjoying the presence of the Messiah. This probably describes the church saints. Meanwhile, on earth, there are many descriptions of the Jewish people responding to the Messiah and accepting Him. But the Church is no longer seen on earth, experiencing the terror of the tribulation age. The Church will return only afterwards, at the Second Coming.

There are some Christians who seem to have a death wish! They almost delight in the thought that they may pass through the horror of that great Holocaust. But the Bible certainly sees it differently. And this truly is our blessed hope!

CONCLUSION

In this brief study we've noted some issues of history and the past. The greatest of the Jewish sages until very recently have looked for the literal coming of Israel's Messiah. Of course, the great difference between Judaism and Christianity is His first coming. The Jewish rabbis, even during the days of Christ, believed everything most Christians believed concerning the son of David. They believed He would be born of a virgin, born of the house of David, born in Bethlehem. They even anticipated His sacrificial death for the world and His resurrection. They believed He would reflect the characteristics of God. He would be a holy and righteous one who existed in times past.

We've also seen that the early church fathers clearly believed these same things and agreed with the Jewish rabbis about the Messiah coming to reign. They looked for a literal return to earth and a thousand-year Kingdom in Jerusalem.

But with St. Augustine in the 4th century, the Church lost this great literal and historical vision. The coming medieval church, with its pomp and ceremony, saw itself as a replacement for the Jewish people. It believed that Israel would no longer be blessed, and that as a scattered people they had no place in God's program.

But now, in the end-times, scholars and laymen alike have been anticipating this earthly Second Coming with all its accompanying fulfillment of Old Testament prophecies.

We believe we are very near and that all the signs are evident.

If this is so, the believer has a great privilege and obligation to live his life in telling others of this great hope of mankind.

Man has virtually destroyed his world, and now faces natural and divine judgment.

Among those studying this booklet, it is possible there are some who have not received Jesus as their Savior and Lord. We trust as you finish this book, you will think carefully about your own relationship to Him. God does not expect perfection, nor does He desire our works to please Him. He asks but simple faith. The Second Coming of Jesus will be a coming for judgment of the world. His first coming was a coming for peace and grace.

"For God so loved the world that He gave up His only-begotten Son, so that whoever believes in Him shall not perish but have eternal life." (John 3:16)

STUDY BOOK SERIES by Zola Levitt

THE MIRACLE OF PASSOVER:

A complete explanation of the beautiful symbols and shadows of the Messiah which appear in this crown jewel of Jewish Holy Days. The true meaning of Communion as the Lord instituted it and as the Church practices it.

THE SPIRIT OF PENTECOST:

From the fear and trembling of the Upper Room to the magnificent miracle of the coming of the Holy Spirit. An exciting presentation of the full meaning of "the birthday of the Church."

A CHRISTIAN LOVE STORY:

The Jewish wedding customs of the Messiah's time and how He fulfilled them all in calling out His Bride, the Church. A new and deeper understanding of the bond between the Bridegroom and each believer — a spiritual "Love Story."

THE SIGNS OF THE END:

The Messiah's own words of warning about the conditions that would prevail in the world at the end of God's plan. Are we now approaching the Great Tribulation and the return of our King?

GLORY: The Future of the Believers:

The entire prophetic system explained for those who are going to live it! The Rapture, our time in Heaven, the Kingdom and Eternity. Where we go from here. Our rewards, our eternal lives, our entire future.

THE SEVEN FEASTS OF ISRAEL:

A complete explanation of the holy days God gave Moses on Mount Sinai, and how each was fulfilled by our Lord. Passover, Pentecost, Trumpets, Tabernacles, etc., fully discussed as to their hidden meanings in the Messiah. A very special section on how every baby in the womb develops according to God's system of the holy days.

THE SECOND COMING:

The prime difference between the biblical faith and worldy religions is that with the Messiah we have a bright future. What we see is not all we get. The life in this world is of little importance to those who have been promised the Kingdom to come. The return of the King fully explained.

SEVEN CHURCHES: Does Yours Fit In?:

A refreshing and unusual perspective on the churches presented in Revelation 2 and 3. A Jewish Christian and Bible scholar, Zola looks at these earliest churches from the Old Testament and Jewish traditional point of view. A highly interesting and most useful study, applicable to church life everywhere today.

HOW CAN A GENTILE BE SAVED?:

Christians always ask Zola, "How did you come to the Lord?" Their **real** question is, "How can a Jew be saved?" He finally decided to make a biblical inquiry into how **they** got saved. The results are extremely thought-provoking.

"IN MY FATHER'S HOUSE":

The Lord said, "In my Father's house are many mansions... I go to prepare a place for you." An explanation of the incredible seven years we will spend as guests in heaven, in the Messiah's Father's house.

ISRAEL, MY PROMISED:

Has God finished with the Jews? Are the modern Israelites the valid Chosen People of the Bible? A sensitive and very personal look at the land of our Lord, as seen today and as promised in the Kingdom.

A current list of Zola Levitt's books, tapes, albums, etc. is available at no charge from:

ZOLA
P.O. Box 12268
Dallas, Texas 75225

Production by:
Great Impressions Printing & Graphics